Oxygen for the
of encouragement...
~Sheila Taormina, Olympic Champion in swimming, World Champion in the triathlon, and World Cup Standings leader in the pentathlon.

Oxygen for the Swimmer
A Breath of Encouragement

**Alexandria Mangas
with
Janet Hommel Mangas**

Copyright © 2009
by Alexandria Mangas with Janet Hommel Mangas

Oxygen for the Swimmer
by Alexandria Mangas with Janet Hommel Mangas

Printed in the United States of America

ISBN 978-1-60791-603-1

All rights reserved solely by the author. The author guarantees all contents are original and do not infringe upon the legal rights of any other person or work. No part of this book may be reproduced in any form without the permission of the author. The views expressed in this book are not necessarily those of the publisher.

Unless otherwise indicated, all Scripture quotations are taken from the HOLY BIBLE, NEW INTERNATIONAL VERSION®. NIV®. Copyright © 1973, 1978, 1984 by International Bible Society. Used by permission of Zondervan. All rights reserved.

Scripture marked The Message is taken from *The Message* by Eugene H. Peterson, copyright © 1993, 1994, 1995, 2000, 2001, 2002. Used by permission of NavPress Publishing Group. All rights reserved.

Scripture marked NLT is taken from the *Holy Bible*, New Living Translation, copyright © 1996. Used by permission of Tyndale House Publishers, Inc., Wheaton, Illinois 60189. All rights reserved.

www.xulonpress.com

Dedication

To my fellow chlorine-soaked swimmers
who persevere through practices all year long.

May your love of God be as solid and present as the
concrete walls within which you swim.

Acknowledgments

I will praise God's name in song and glorify him with thanksgiving.

Psalm 69:30

I would also like to thank everyone who helped bring this book to fruition:

- Joyce Long – for the subtitle suggestion and a pool full of encouragement.

- Dad, Chloe, and Phoebe – for listening to story after story and giving critique on our annual twenty-one-hour road trip to fish at Sandy Beach Lodge in Red Lake, Canada.

- Dr. Dennis Hensley – for encouraging me, sending material to read, and telling me that I wasn't too young to publish a book.

- Coach Craig Bauer – for instilling a love of swimming into my soul the past nine years and being Christ-like.

- Christianna Parell, Kaity Chappelow, Lori Nichols, Libby Weldon, and all my fellow USA teammates since elementary school– thanks for all the good memories we shared on team-building canoe trips, during divisionals, and while pasta loading.

- Covenant Christian High School Swim Team – for becoming my sisters and brothers for seventeen weeks out of the year and making the plunge into cold water at 5:30 every morning.

- A big thank you to all our contributing authors and their families — *I thank my God every time I remember you* – (Philippians 1:3).

Table of Contents

Introduction xiii

Section 1 — Overcoming 15

Swimming Heroes – Learning from the Masters	Alexandria Mangas	17
The Goliath Complex	Craig Bauer	21
Kick Like Barbie, Breathe in My Armpit	Elisabeth Nicholson	25
Swimming Heroes	Nate Tauzer	27

Section 2 — What I Learned from Swimming That Has Nothing to Do with Water 31

The Greatest Lesson	Sheila Taormina	33
Inspiration	Cindy Kalinoski	35
Learning Valuable Lessons	Elena Patton	39
You Can't Please Everyone	Kathy Pride	43
More Than Pink Ribbons	Laura Stufflebam	47

Section 3 — Poolside Life Lessons 51

Hard Work	Jessica Long, 2008 Beijing Gold Medalist....................53
A Swim Mom Who Didn't Jump In	Janet Hommel Mangas.......57
The Loud Coach	Allison Lanese 61
Swimming with the Ten-and-Unders as a Teen	Kathy Pride 65

Section 4 — Poolside Stories: Families, Friends, and Teammates 69

The Swim Lesson	Bryan Schalesky as told to Marlo Schalesky................71
The Near Miss	Kate Wilt 75
Rest for the Weary – Prerace Fuel	Kathy Pride 79
The Far Side of the Pool	Marlo Schalesky................81

Section 5 — DQ'd..85

Jesus "Walking on Water" Swim Meet Cartoon	Cuyler Black 87
Playing by the Rules	Kathy Pride 89
My First Swim Meet at Eight Years Old	Alexandria Mangas............91

Section 6 — Hearing His Voice in the Water 93

What God Has to Say	Moire Yue...........................95
My Prayer Closet Is 25 Yards Long	Beverly Bush Smith 99
Am I a Swimmer?	Melanie LeBaron 103
A Breath of Encouragement	Judith Ann Squier............107

A Final Letter to His
    Senior Swimmers   Coach Jon Lederhouse 111

Section 7 — A Swim-bag Full of Goodies 115

Top Ten Q&A with Olympic Gold Medalist Sheila
    Taormina (with Alexandria Mangas) 117
Are You a Swimming Genius? (Take the swimming
    trivia quiz to find out) 121
Swim Quotes for Your Locker 125
Great Bible Verses to Memorize While Swimming 127

Introduction

Two years before the 2008 Beijing Olympics, the idea for *Oxygen for the Swimmer — A Breath of Encouragement* rippled from a car conversation on the way to swim practice. The question left us without an answer: Why do swimmers never acknowledge God in most popular swim magazines and websites? We began searching for books or even articles that combined both a love of swimming and love of our heavenly Father and Creator.

This book is a humble offering to fill the gap. Just as a swimmer longs to fill his lungs with oxygen, and must continue to do so, we hope the words in this book fill you with encouragement.

Jesus answered, "It is written:
'Man does not live on bread alone, but on every word that
comes from the mouth of God.'"

Matthew 4:4

Section 1
Overcoming

James 1:2-4

*Consider it pure joy, my brothers, whenever you face
trials of many kinds,
because you know that the testing of your faith
develops perseverance.
Perseverance must finish its work so that you
may be mature and complete,
not lacking anything.*

There are over 42,000 Master swimmers in the
United States–what lifelong lessons
can we learn sitting at the flippers of the Masters?

SWIMMING HEROES —
LEARNING FROM THE MASTERS
Alexandria Mangas
Indiana High School Swimmer

I had the blessing of seeing Michelle McKeehan break the national record in the 200 IM at the 2007 Indiana State High School Finals. I was sitting with her team when she finished with a time of 1:58:06, and every person in the packed Indianapolis natatorium stood and gave her a cheering ovation, including all of her high school rival opponents. It was awesome when the loudspeaker boomed, "Michelle McKeehan has just broken the 200 IM national record." I had many heroes that day.

In this same Indianapolis natatorium the summer of 2006, as I volunteered for the Masters championship swim meet, I witnessed a hero that didn't even break a record. She wasn't as muscular as Michelle or as toned, but she had a slight swimmer's quadricep defined line down her leg. She didn't have the packed natatorium or the press all over her, but she had the attention of everyone in the room. She didn't have a coach to support her, but she did have two teammates support her on the block for the start. She was my hero that day and every day since. Never have I seen a more moving picture as I watched her hobble toward the block on crutches with a smile spread across her wrinkled face. When I checked her in for her event I found out she was 80 years old. As she made her way to the block, a younger swimmer came up and took her crutches, while two other swimmers assisted her up on the block and held her to balance her for the start. When the starter beep sounded, the other competing swimmers pushed off with their strong legs and dove in for a fast start. After her block assistants let go of her, my young-at-heart competitor gracefully fell into the water and began to swim.

She made it down 25 meters and was finishing back slowly, freestyling her way down the pool, when toward the end I thought *she isn't going to make it*. As I looked around deciding what to do, I saw other panic-stricken faces.

Then I heard a yell.

The first yell was followed by another yell, and soon a tidal wave of contagious cheers erupted from swimmers surrounding the pool. Standing in her honor, cheering and clapping, every swimmer on deck, every timer, and every person in the Indianapolis natatorium rose to their feet encouraging her to finish. And she did finish. I recorded her time, though it was irrelevant—everyone at the natatorium that day knew she was a winner. Even while being helped out of the pool, as winded as she was, she wore a smile on her face. It was that day that I realized heroes come in all sizes, ages, and speeds.

May the God who gives endurance and encouragement give you a spirit of unity among yourselves as you follow Christ Jesus, so that with one heart and mouth you may glorify the God and Father of our Lord Jesus Christ. — Romans 15:5-6

Aly Mangas is currently a high school senior in Indianapolis and loves swimming. She plans to continue her swimming career in college. Her favorite event is the 200 butterfly and swimming distance. You can contact her at oxygenfortheswimmer@yahoo.com.

THE GOLIATH COMPLEX
Craig Bauer

While attending my first year in college, rumor had it I would be swimming the 100-yard freestyle. As I started training I quickly realized I needed much improvement. The long distances the coach gave me to swim were too long for the intervals. My sprinting was not fast enough. At least that was my thinking at the time. Day after day and week after week went by, and I was still training with the same results. Or so I thought. Little did I know I was being trained to swim against a guy who had never been beat in the 100-yard freestyle in his college career. His name was John Nunnally, although they should have said his name was Goliath. Just the thought of having to swim against a swimmer who always won just shook me up. But I kept training with one thought in the back of my mind: *This is going to be a disaster.* I gave myself the Goliath complex.

To me the Goliath complex is looking at your competition as being so big you can't win. In my case I was seeing John Nunnally as Goliath, so big he couldn't lose.

I was attending a Christian college that required all its students to take a Bible class every semester. Being the first semester, I was taking New Testament Survey. It just happened that our professor brought up Philippians 4:13, which says, "I can do all things through him who strengthens me." It turned my head and training around.

Let me jump ahead to the day of the race. The natatorium was small so it seemed packed with the amount of spectators allowed in. The pool was also small: a four-lane, 20-yard pool. That's right, I had to swim five lengths for the 100-yard freestyle. The last heat mounted the all-wood starting blocks that had carpet on the top to prevent splinters and slipping. Everyone became quiet and the starter said in his slow voice "take your mark." The gun sounded and the race was on. I entered the water and came to a point in the first length where I could see Goliath—I mean John—swimming next to me. We turned together and we stroked together. I was told after the heat that it looked like we had choreographed the entire race. Five lengths of stroke-for-stroke and turn-for-turn. We came to our fourth turn and I, or should I say we, came out of our turn together and started our last 20 yards of synchronized swimming. My chest was pounding, my shoulders were numb, and all I could hear was water running past my ears. As I approached the wall all I could remember was to keep my head down and go for the wall. I did just that and beat John Nunnally, the guy who *can* be beat.

As I look back on the experience, it proves to me what David must have thought standing there in front of Goliath. He had God on his side, so David did not see Goliath as being too big to hit, he saw Goliath as being too big to miss. I guess it was the same with John Goliath Nunnally.

A champion named Goliath, who was from Gath, came out of the Philistine camp. He was over nine feet tall. He had a bronze helmet on his head and wore a coat of scale armor of bronze weighing five thousand shekels; on his legs he wore bronze greaves, and a bronze javelin was slung on his back. His spear shaft was like a weaver's rod, and its iron point weighed six hundred shekels. — 1 Samuel 17:4-6

David said to the Philistine, "You come against me with sword and spear and javelin, but I come against you in the name of the LORD Almighty, the God of the armies of Israel, whom you have defied." — 1 Samuel 17:45

As the Philistine moved closer to attack him, David ran quickly toward the battle line to meet him. Reaching into his bag and taking out a stone, he slung it and struck the Philistine on the forehead. The stone sank into his forehead, and he fell facedown on the ground. — 1 Samuel 17:48-49

Craig Bauer is the coach of the Covenant Christian High School Warrior Swim Team in Indianapolis, Indiana. He previously coached the Mooresville, Indiana, community swim team, the USA Southwest Indy Stingrays, for eight years. A collegiate swimmer at Harding University, he currently trains with the United States Masters Swim Club, Indy Swim Fit (ISF), and competes when he's not coaching. During the Fort Lauderdale YMCA Masters Nationals at the Hall of Fame Pool in 2002, he noted: "I was lucky enough to be a part of a 200-medley relay team that broke the Masters national record 1:44:59 — it stood for two years."

As a coach, Bauer believes in leading by example through commitment. "I try to create an environment of fun, teamwork, and sportsmanship. I encourage swimmers to set goals and participate in swimming for a lifetime."

Kick Like Barbie, Breathe in My Armpit
Elisabeth Nicholson (18)

Competitive swimming is so different from the swimming done at a pool party. Unfortunately, two years ago that was the only notion I had of swimming. Walking onto the deck my sophomore year in high school was a blind step for me. Fortunately, my sarcastic nature accompanied me through the season, offering a unique outlet for my stress. I recorded all of my thoughts in a notebook, hoping to one day look back and see how inept I used to be. On Saturday, November 11, 2005, I reflected upon my practice that morning. "Today I learned to flip turn. I started out doing handstands; however, I eventually was able to do a complete somersault. They are quite fun when I don't get water up my nose of course! Next, we moved on to diving. I worked for forty minutes in the deep end and got a pretty good handle on the technique. Once I got back to the lanes, I became very nervous about hitting the bottom of the shallow pool. Jumping off the side, I found it to be just fine. When starting from the blocks, however, things did not go so gracefully. After seven belly flops, practice ended. My entire front side is red and chafed. I cannot feel anything anymore. Can't wait to repeat all of this at next practice!"

It is so difficult sometimes to continue working and practicing when the only fruit of labor seems to be pain. I certainly felt that way about starts. Hard work in practice does pay off though. Personally, I have come so far from that first year of swimming. Now in my senior year, I am by no means the perfect swimmer. In fact, my starting techniques still could use a little bit of work, but I have improved so much since that very first belly flop.

"I think I am finally getting 'the feel' for freestyle. Kick like Barbie, breathe in my armpit, and keep my eyes open." – Written in Elisabeth Nicholson's journal on the second day of practice

Elisabeth Nicholson is a freshman at Butler University majoring in pre-med and Spanish, with plans to become a doctor. An award-winning equestrian, she started swimming in high school, which opened her eyes to a strange new sport. She encourages anyone interested in swimming that it is never too late. Her advice: "Don't forget to kick like Barbie and breathe in your armpit."

SWIMMING HEROES
Nate Tauzer (18)
2008 Paralympian Trial Contender

Standing on the block, I look out across the pool. On my left is a man without a leg, and on the right another man without a hand. A chill runs through me as I question my reasons for being in this line of characters. After all, I have no missing limbs or any obvious handicaps. I look at the pure determination on their faces, and it makes me remember my own struggles. I remember doctors telling my mom I might never walk. I think back on the eight weeks of intense training that it took to get here. A buzzer sounds—my mind goes blank except for the thought *go fast!*

I am Nate Tauzer, a homeschooled kid who has mild cerebral palsy. I graduated from high school in 2006. The summer between high school and college was going to be different: no work, no worries; just sit back and dream about college in the fall. After one week I was bored and spending most of my time on computer games.

My summer and my life changed with one phone call from my former swim coach and counselor, Pat Riser.

"Nate, I have seen you swim and think you could qualify as a Paralympian."

The Paralympics are like the Olympics but are designed for people with physical disabilities. In eight weeks the Pan Am games were going to be held in San Antonio, Texas, where the best swimmers from around the world—mostly from the U.S., Canada, and Mexico—would compete. Athletes would also be classified by a rating level of being physically challenged. In order to qualify for the meet, I needed to swim 34 seconds in the 50-meter freestyle at an approved USA swim meet. I had not swum for about a year. My first official time was 54 seconds in the 50-meter free. I needed to drop 20 seconds in seven weeks. I trained hard and dropped 5 seconds but still had 15 more seconds to drop. By the sixth week, with only weeks to go, I swam a 35-second fifty.

My last meet was the Junior Olympic Meet held in Davis, California. It was record-breaking heat in an outdoor pool. The temperature was 113 degrees, poolside was 122 degrees, and the pool water felt like a hot tub at 91 degrees. Of course, my event was at 3:15 p.m.—one of the last events. I needed a 34-second 50 to qualify. I swam a personal best of 34:34, but it was not good enough to qualify. Showing me support, my team decided to let me swim in the 400 freestyle relay replacing one of their best swimmers, giving me one last chance. I still couldn't make the time. Phone calls began flying and the organizers decided to let me go and compete so I could at least be classified. That's how I got to San Antonio.

As I walked onto the deck of the huge indoor Olympic pool, I saw the usual array of towels, clothes, and swim gear. But also piled among the debris were prosthetic feet, arms, legs, wheelchairs, canes, and other unrecognizable pieces of paraphernalia. One man looked as if he were swimming upside down at first glance until I realized his foot was connected backwards to his leg. I noticed a man swimming with only one arm, another with no feet or hands, and a woman with no limbs at all. I couldn't stop myself from thinking, *What the heck am I doing here?* Sure my legs hurt, but I have all my arms and legs, and I walk without a cane or the use of a wheelchair. It was hard to imagine that I deserved to be classified with people who had overcome so much to be here.

I showed up at my classification time five minutes early and waited half an hour. I finally went in with my mom, who was my official manager, and met the four assessors. Each individual who is assessed has an assessor from their own country, and three other assessors representing three other countries. They are all medical professionals, generally doctors or physical therapists with training in working with physically challenged athletes. They had me wave around my legs, arms, and hands, and I thought maybe they were trying to figure out which ones were fake. They put me in the pool to swim for about twenty minutes and then went to decide how to classify me.

The classification is on a scale of 1 to 10, 1 being the most disabled and 10 being the most able-bodied. There are three parts: the first number is your freestyle classification, the second number is breaststroke, and the third number is IM. IM is the lowest number on your classification. When they handed me my classification of 9.8.8, I was shocked and actually a little mad. My mom was slightly relieved that they could classify me, yet sad that I really was classified as disabled. It was the assessors' turn to be shocked when I bluntly asked why I was classified so low. Most competitors want to be classified as low as possible to have the best advantage in competition. I was so insulted when they told me it was my coordination level that lowered my score that I cross-examined them: "Do you mean you think I am uncoordinated?" Later, my new buddy who lost his leg to bone cancer at fourteen and has a classification of 9.9.9, teased me: "You're more disabled than a one-legged man."

I then embarked on one of the most important journeys of my life, as I am now training at an elite level to make the 2008 Paralympic Games in Beijing, China. And when I begin to struggle I remember: *Use what I have, not that which I have missing.*

I praise you because I am fearfully and wonderfully made; your works are wonderful, I know that full well. – Psalm 139:14

Although Nate Tauzer didn't make it to Beijing 2008, his dream of Paralympics is alive and well. He is training in San Diego with PASD and hopes to make the 2012 London games. He is currently getting certified in massage therapy and plans to start a business working with professional athletes.

Section 2
What I Learned from Swimming That Has Nothing to Do with Water

Deuteronomy 32:2

*Let my teaching fall like rain and my words
descend like dew,
like showers on new grass,
like abundant rain on tender plants.*

THE GREATEST LESSON
Sheila Taormina
Olympic Gold Medalist in the 1996 Atlanta Olympics
2000 & 2004 Olympic Triathlete
2008 Olympic Pentathlete

The greatest lesson I learned in sports that relates to life came from two back-to-back Olympics in two different sports. In 1996 I was part of the 4 x 200 freestyle relay that won gold in Atlanta. Jenny Thompson anchored that relay, and as she was coming to the wall for the gold medal, I looked up at the twenty-five people from my family in the stands. They were jumping up and down with excitement and I thought, *How cool to have the entire family here and to win in my home country. Look at how much fun everyone is having.*

Then in 2000, I made the Olympic team for the triathlon on the other side of the world in Sydney, Australia. As I was coming to the finish of the race I was in sixth place, with no way to catch fifth place and no way seventh place could catch me. I could cruise to the finish line, but there would be no medal this time. About 200 meters from the finish line was my family—twenty of them flew all the way to Australia to be together. As I passed by them, they were jumping up and down going wild just as they had in 1996. At that moment I understood that relationships are the most important thing in life. My relationships with family, with God, and with good friends never change based on the outcome. I am blessed to have such people in my life.

A faithful friend is the medicine of life. – Ecclesiastes 6:16

Sheila Taormina became the first female athlete in the 112-year history of the modern Games to compete in four Olympics in three different sports. She represented the USA as an Olympic gold champion in the 4 x 200 meter freestyle relay at the 1996 Atlanta Games, triathlon (sixth place) in the 2000 Sydney Games, triathlon in the 2004 Athens Games, and in the pentathlon at the 2008 Beijing Games, in which she placed first in two of the five events: swimming and equestrian show jumping. Events of the modern pentathlon include air pistol shooting, epee fencing, 200-meter swim, stadium show jumping, and 3-kilometer run. Sheila, an Olympic champion in swimming, World Champion in the triathlon, and World Cup standings leader in the pentathlon, is also a unique motivational speaker. Check out her blog at http://www.SheliaT.com

INSPIRATION
Cindy Kalinoski

It was 7:30 a.m. and they still weren't there. Maybe no one else noticed, but I did. I looked for this pair every time I swam. Freezing cold winters, they were there. Steamy summers found them at their table in the lobby next to the window by the pool. Every time I went, there they were. But today the table sat empty.

As I struggled through my workout, doing a sidestroke on this lap, I wondered about them and why their disappearance fazed me. After all, they were just two older ladies sharing breakfast at the Y.

Although I knew Norma, I didn't even know her friend's name. But they were so faithful. I watched their friendship. Each morning I noticed they went their separate ways, Norma down to the pool and her friend upstairs to the YWORKS gym. Then they'd meet and have their cereal together before starting their day. Every day. The day Norma turned eighty, I saw her friend give her a card and a present.

There was something so compelling about their companionship. I guess I found it reassuring somehow. And God knew I needed reassurance. I needed inspiration to get up every morning, and I needed inspiration to venture outdoors to the Y and hop in the pool. With fibromyalgia, morning pain is a given. In the dead of winter, when it's dark and the cold exacerbates my stiffness, mornings can be a real challenge. I'm often tempted to stay in bed, but I know that would just make it hurt worse. Only swimming in the warm pool helped, and often each motion hurt and made me wonder if it was worth it. So I guess it's not surprising that I was uplifted by the faithfulness of two friends who left their warm homes every morning, worked out, and visited. If they could make it, I could too. So where were they today?

As I took my last backstroke lap, I sensed movement in the window and glanced over. I smiled as I recognized Norma and her friend, taking off their coats and settling down with their cereal bowls. All was well. I would come back later this week, and next week, and the week after that. I just needed a little faithfulness as an example. And while they had no idea I counted on them, I like to think that Norma and her friend were somehow blessed because they helped me start my day. I know I was.

Therefore we do not lose heart. Though outwardly we are wasting away, yet inwardly we are being renewed day by day. For our light and momentary troubles are achieving for us an eternal glory that far outweighs them all. So we fix our eyes not on what is seen, but on what is unseen. For what is seen is temporary, but what is unseen is eternal.
— 2 Corinthians 4:16-18

Cindy Kalinoski discovered the benefits of swimming six years ago and can't imagine ever stopping. As TheWordHelper.com in Pennsylvania, she provides The English Makeover seminar, web content, writing, editing, copywriting, and proofreading services. Her work appears regularly in *Susquehanna Style* magazine and *BusinessVOICE*. God recently led her to Ethiopia for an amazing week of work and fellowship with AIDS widows.

LEARNING VALUABLE LESSONS
Elena Patton

The early morning drive to a dual swim meet is always tense. It is often filled with anxiety and tension, not just because you are competing for placement, but because you are competing for points for your team. The morning of one particular meet was a cold November day, and since my entire family was going to the meet I decided to ride with them instead of taking the team bus. We pulled up and parked in front of the Y, directly behind the coach bus. This would ensure that when it was all loaded, we could be the first ones to follow it.

The bus soon pulled out of the lot and was on its way. My family and I were talking and enjoying our ride. Every now and then I would glance up to make sure the coach bus was still in sight. Although this was not a pool we had been to before, we were following the team so we put away our Mapquest and relied on the bus ahead of us to lead us to our destination. About an hour into the trip, we decided to make a quick stop and get something to drink. We watched as the bus took the next exit, and after we had gotten our drinks we pulled out and were once again behind it.

Soon another hour had gone by and we were starting to wonder if we would ever get there. However, we decided there was nothing to worry about. "They can't start the meet until the team gets there," we joked. It was just then that the bus took an unexpected turn and pulled into a mall parking lot. We sat there puzzled, wondering why they were detouring, and we started making jokes about who might have forgotten their suit or lost their goggles.

Quite unexpectedly the bus driver stepped out of the bus and began to check all the compartments. We noticed he was studying us with a rather puzzled look. I finally decided to run up to the bus to see just why they had stopped. As I approached the driver, I made the shocking discovery that there was no one aboard—we had been following the wrong bus for well over an hour.

Panic swept over us as we frantically looked for our Mapquest to determine not only where we were going, but where we were. We quickly hit the road and retraced our path. After several stops, we found our way to the pool just in time for the first event. Although I had missed warm-up, I knew my heart was racing fast enough to set a new pool record.

I learned several valuable lessons that day. Sometimes it's not how fast you swim but how fast you can rebound when things don't go the way you expect. Second, sometimes you have to be able to laugh, even at yourself. And perhaps most importantly, keep your eyes on the finish and not just the bus.

It is not good to have zeal without knowledge, nor to be hasty and miss the way. – Proverbs 19:2

Elena Patton, age fifteen, was born in Sevastopol, Ukraine. She now lives in Pennsylvania and is surrounded by family and friends who love and encourage her to fulfill her dreams. She has been swimming for the Y for four years and loves the butterfly and freestyle distance events. She enjoys hanging out with close friends at meets and cheering her teammates on.

YOU CAN'T PLEASE EVERYONE
Kathy Pride

I shook my head and rolled my eyes in exasperation. Complain, complain, complain. If there were so many people who knew better, then why were my husband and I the only two coaches?

"She doesn't swim backstroke," "Swimming isn't the only thing she does, you know...," "My daughter can only make practice twice a week and we won't be coming to the away meets, that's just too far to go," and my personal favorite, "Why isn't my son leading the lane?"

I had been warned but I blew off the admonition. After all, I was one of the coaches, there to work with the kids, so I didn't pay much attention when my friend Sue warned me about the parents.

"You'll never make the parents happy, you'll see," she said. I cocked my head to the side, a quizzical look on my face. "What do you mean?" I asked. After all, I had the perfect situation. My husband and I were coaching Y swimming, our boys were swimming, and we were all in the same place at the same time. Now how often did that happen? We loved working with the kids and seeing their improvement while building a winning program that emphasized team performance and individual improvement. Life couldn't be better—or could it?

It could if the parents would simply allow us to be coaches. My friend was right; we weren't winning popularity contests with the parents. I have to admit I hadn't given much thought to the parents when we took over leadership of the floundering team. The group was desperate for coaches, and at first the parents were welcoming and relieved that the program had survived. Then slowly the muttering began. It reminded me of the quip about individuals becoming pediatricians or teachers because they loved kids and then burning out because they had such a hard time dealing with the parents.

Then the phone started to ring. "Why isn't Joey in four events?" came the first demanding question. Soon the phone rang again. "I don't want Sally in all those relays; she needs to be swimming individual events" came another complaint. Winning as a team was fine as long as it didn't require individual sacrifice.

What happened to teamwork, camaraderie, improved times, and a winning record? This was a competitive swim program after all. But Sue had been right, we would never make everyone happy, and a cloud of complaints settled over our family togetherness on the pool deck.

We learned a lot over the years we coached swimming. Most of it was about swimming, but one of the most valuable lessons was that no matter what you do, you can't please everyone. And that's okay.

He who scorns instruction will pay for it, but he who respects a command is rewarded. — Proverbs 13:13.

Kathy Pride wears many hats, including the stressed-out diva tiara (www.divacelebration.com) and bathing cap as a triathlete and Masters swimmer. She lives in central Pennsylvania with her husband and four children where she blogs daily at www.kathypride.com. She is also an encourager, writer, and speaker. Join the conversation!

MORE THAN PINK RIBBONS
Laura Stufflebam

Growing up, I loved swimming. My mom called me a waterdog nearly from birth, and while I was, as she said, "pretty in the water," I wasn't fast — at all. A dying turtle probably could have passed me in the water. As a result of my gracefully lethargic strokes, I was never chosen to swim in *real* races during our summertime swim meets, but my coach always made sure to include me in the exhibition races, the ones where you get a nice, happy, pink participation ribbon.

I hated those pink ribbons. The message they sent me time and time again was that I wasn't enough. I wasn't fast enough. I wasn't good enough to swim in a real race for a real ribbon. How I longed to just once have a blue, red, or white ribbon to hang on my wall instead of those mocking pink ones. I wanted to prove that I was a contributing member of the team, that I could win points instead of always feeling like the side-ring circus show to provide entertainment for the crowd while the true athletes rested up for their big races.

Oxygen for the Swimmer

The summer I turned thirteen my mom suggested I teach swim lessons to earn a little money of my own. In my head, it was a simple case of "those who can't do, teach," but I was thrilled to discover that I *liked* teaching much more than I ever liked racing.

One summer, an anxious young mother brought her eight-year-old son to me. Alex, like so many of my other students, had tried group lessons at the public pool, but he had been pushed off the diving board and hadn't immediately popped back up. The lifeguard had to go in after him, and that memory now paralyzed him. He would swim with friends at the country club, but he wouldn't follow them into the deep end. Alex's mom had heard several stories of my success with fearful swimmers and thought I might be able to help. For two weeks we worked on perfecting his already quite-passable technique, and I made a deal with Alex: if at the end of our two weeks he would go off the diving board, I'd buy him a candy bar. (Kids will do almost anything for a Tootsie Roll!)

Each day I had to reassure Alex he would be fine and that I would be right beside him as we painstakingly crossed the short incline separating deep from shallow waters. Even though I could see the longing in his eyes, the wish to be able to join his friends laughing and playing in the deep end, he struggled daily in an understandable tension between these desires and near panic at what would happen if he tried and failed.

Finally, on the last day of our session, I had Alex's favorite candy bar waiting on the table when he arrived. As he walked through the screen door, his eyes immediately fixed on the prize. I could see his mouth watering. His eyes swung to the diving board, weighing his decision. As he shrugged off his street clothes, I could see him trembling from head to toe, and I heard his mother quietly ask my mom, "What am

I going to do if he doesn't come up again? I'll never get him back in the water!"

We warmed up, swimming back and forth across the incline. When he made it to the far edge of the incline, he looked at me, eyes wide with trepidation, to see if I'd make him go any farther.

"Wanna try the diving board?"

A quick glance back to the candy bar was all he needed, and a single nod had him scurrying toward the ladder. As he made his way to the board, I kept assuring him I would be right there. I would catch him if anything went wrong, and I was positive he was going to do great. He took a shuddering breath, heaving his chest as only an eight-year-old can, and with one last look at the promised candy bar, he closed his eyes and jumped in. I knew his mother and mine were both holding their breath. I was too.

Suddenly, Alex crashed through the surface. His face was priceless—radiant from defeating his fear. Both our mothers were on their feet cheering and crying as he splashed around, reveling in the wonder of being completely suspended in water. The waiting candy bar was the last thing on anyone's mind.

In that moment, I knew a shelf full of pink ribbons didn't matter anymore. Who cared if I was slower than molasses in a race? I had just helped a little boy overcome a fear that could have plagued him for years. I finally understood that I had more to offer the swimming world than just a plethora of pink ribbons and a good laugh. I could teach! For many young swimmers just like Alex, I made an impact I never could have made from a starting block.

No, I decided, pink ribbons mean nothing at all.

"The task of the excellent teacher is to stimulate 'apparently ordinary' people to unusual effort. The tough problem is not in identifying winners: it is in making winners out of ordinary people." ~K. Patricia Cross

Section 3
Poolside Life Lessons

2 Timothy 1:7

For God did not give us a spirit of timidity, but a spirit of power, of love and of self-discipline.

A Letter to You About Hard Work

Jessica Long
Long won four gold medals in the 2008 Beijing Paralympics:
in the 100 butterfly, 100 freestyle, 200 individual medley, and 400 free.
She also won silver in the 100 backstroke and bronze in the 100 breaststroke.
2006 Paralympian of the Year

Since both of my legs were amputated below the knees when I was eighteen months old, I have always had to work extra hard just to keep up with the other kids. There was no time to waste feeling sorry for myself. While everyone else could run up the hill, I had to practice repeatedly just to be able to walk up the hill. I fell down trying so many times I lost count, but after each fall I picked myself up and tried again. Finally, I conquered the hill.

It's been like that with every physical activity I have tried. I have had to overcome challenges in gymnastics, basketball, rock climbing, skiing, ice skating, and even learning to run and ride a bike. I remember my first time skiing when the ski lift started and my prosthetic legs fell off. I looked back to see several confused people looking at my boots and skis sitting upright in the snow with my legs still sticking up out of them.

Through it all, I have discovered there is no substitute for determination and hard work. If you want to be successful at anything, you have to get up when you fall down and never, never, never give up.

Swimming is no exception. It takes hard work to be successful. I was ten years old when I first joined a swim team, and I couldn't do all the strokes. The butterfly was especially difficult because I felt I would drown before reaching the other end of the pool. It took a lot of practice and hard work, but I now hold world records in all four strokes (including the fly, now my favorite stroke).

Swimming is perhaps the sport that requires the most work of all. I have heard it said that other sports (football, soccer, lacrosse, track, etc.) only exist because people who can't make the swim team need something else to do. Maybe the reason why swimming is thought of in this way is not only that it takes stamina, but because it takes so very long to get good at it. Most people don't stick with it long enough to excel. It requires too much effort for most. That's one of the reasons I like swimming, because it takes hard work to get good at it. Everyone has it within them to put forth what it requires. They only have to make the decision and do it. So whether you're going for your personal best time or a world record, work hard at it and you will eventually reach your goal if you remain determined and persistent.

Also, make sure you are not discouraged by the progress of other people. Concentrate on doing your best even if it may be taking longer than others. I heard of a man who was paralyzed and confined to a wheelchair. When he first started dressing himself it took him four hours. With many attempts and hard work, he was able to reduce that time down to forty-five minutes. For most of us, taking forty-five minutes to get dressed is nothing to get excited about, but for this man it was a personal best time and a whole lot better than four hours. To him it was like a world record.

No matter the challenges you have to overcome, if you work hard at doing your best you can be proud of your accomplishments. So swim hard and work hard and you too will get a personal best time that seems like a world record to you!

Wishing you much hard work in your future....

Jessica Long
May 15, 2008

All hard work brings a profit, but mere talk leads only to poverty. – Proverbs 14:23

A SWIM MOM WHO DIDN'T JUMP IN

Janet Hommel Mangas

She struggled in the water trying to finish the final lap of her 100. Everyone could see her body losing form after her flip turn at the wall. She only had half a pool length to go, but she hesitated, pulled her head out of the water to search for familiar faces in the stands, and hung onto the lane ropes. She was instantly disqualified for the race.

Darting through hundreds of faces in the stands, her eyes frantically connected with the one set of eyes that had protected and encouraged her since her birth seven years before. From 300 yards away, I saw her mouth the word "Mommy." I knew she had tears welling up under her swim goggles.

I wondered if her asthma had flared up and she could not breathe.

She took her eyes off mine and listened to the words of her USA swim coach and her father, who were both on the deck. They were trying to teach her a lesson she would use the rest of her life.

My impulse was to wade through the rows of other parents, jump over the rails and seven feet down onto the deck, then dive from the center-side of the pool under four rows of swim lane ropes. My impulse was to swim, piggybacking my daughter like a koala with her eleven-month-old joey on her back. Even natural swimmers like a baby beaver, which can swim minutes after birth, and are skillful swimmers within a week, are carried on their mother's back when they tire. Nevertheless, deep under my primal motherly instincts, I knew my little offspring needed to learn a more important lesson that she would use the rest of her life.

I heard her pleading to her coach and father to let her swim under the four lane ropes so she could escape the pool from the middle. I knew her father, who cut her umbilical cord at her birth, washed her, and held her like only a father can, wanted to say yes. Her coach, an older and wiser swim coach and father, said, "Phoebe, you can do this." Her coach knew she needed to learn the lesson all athletes must learn and use the rest of their lives.

My furrowed eyes met my husband's. He knew what I was thinking, without the utterance of any words. "Maybe she wasn't ready for this race. Maybe she'll never want to swim again. Maybe her bronchial tubes are closing and she can't breathe." Without words of his own, my husband nodded once and gave me the flat-downward palm, which means: "I love her as much as you — she'll be okay." Her father knew she needed to learn an important lesson — a lesson that sometimes daddies teach best. A lesson that her life depended on.

Her coach and father walked down the pool deck toward the end of the pool where she must finish — with expectation. I stood and cheered her on, "Go, Phoebe!" One by one, the other coaches and parents in the swim bleacher began to stand and applaud.

The village knew this one child must learn an important lesson that she would use the rest of her life. Each one of the villagers knew his cheers and applause could help carry Phoebe to her destination.

As the crowd erupted into standing applause and cheers, she swam to the end of the pool and jumped out to the applause of a lifetime. Phoebe had learned the lesson we must all learn. Whether you finish first or last — always, always, always finish strong.

Note: Four years later, Phoebe continues to laugh and love life — and yes, she loves to swim. She was frightened that day by the underwater speakers, which were booming music and voices during the races— a phenomenon she was not expecting and had not experienced before.

His master replied, "Well done, good and faithful servant! You have been faithful with a few things; I will put you in charge of many things. Come and share your master's happiness!" — Matthew 25:21

Janet Hommel Mangas is a family humor columnist for *The Daily Journal* in Johnson County, Indiana, and the third of seven children. Her father Frank Hommel is the eldest of eleven and her grandfather Ralph Hommel is the youngest of eleven children. Married to an adventurous chiropractor, Dr. Steve Mangas, Janet has been scuba diving in the Cayman Islands, skiing and rappelling in the Colorado mountains, and on mission trips to India and Mexico to build an orphanage with Casas por Cristo. Janet and Steve have three swimming daughters: Aly, eighteen; Chloe, sixteen; and Phoebe, twelve. She would love to hear from you at Oxygenfortheswimmer@yahoo.com.

Coaches not only impart swim techniques, but life lessons

THE LOUD COACH
Allison Lanese (17)

Tears streamed down my face as my mom helped me to slip the black swim cap over my long brown hair. I was dreading practice that day because of the new coach, Kevin. He often raised his voice and did not accept any excuses, and at age nine I did not know how to handle that type of pressure. My mom assured me I would be fine, and I slowly walked toward the pool entrance, trying to wipe the tears from my eyes.

I pried open the heavy white door and slipped inside. I scanned the swimmer-filled deck hoping that Kevin was absent that day, or permanently, but I soon spotted him standing on the brown tile, the extremely curved bill of his old baseball cap casting frightening shadows onto his slightly unshaven face. The shadows hid his eyes, and his mouth was curved in an eerie smile that sent chills down my spine. I shakily pulled my goggles from my bag, trying to hold back the wave of tears welling up behind my eyes and hoping he would not see me. He did. He started yelling at me to get over to my lane and stop being such a baby. I grabbed my bag and bolted from the pool. I ran to the car and begged my mother, between sobs, to take me back home.

That evening as my mom and I were reading together, we came upon a story about an athlete who had a knee injury that restricted her ability to play for long periods of time. Her coach called her a wimp, but she did not let that get to her. I thought about the story as I fell asleep that night.

The next day as my mother drove me to the pool I thought about the story again, and I realized that Kevin was not in charge of my feelings, I was. With this new realization fresh in my mind, I threw open the door and proudly marched into the pool area and inhaled the chlorine smell. With my jaw clenched in determination, I tossed my bag onto the bleachers. I ignored the evil stare of Kevin as I slipped my goggles over my unwavering eyes and leaped into the pool. The cool water embraced and energized me, giving me the extra encouragement I needed to wash away my fears. As I swam down the pool I realized how much I loved swimming and that no one could take that away from me. I survived that practice and the thousands of swim practices since then by constantly believing in myself and not letting anyone try to tell me I am not strong enough. No one can take that self-esteem away from me, not even a loud coach.

"Actions speak louder than coaches."
~Speedo advertisement

"Decide that you want it more than you are afraid of it."
~Bill Cosby

Allison Lanese is a senior at Shaker Heights High School in Ohio. A competitive swimmer for the Shaker Sharks since the first grade, she also competes on her high school's swim team. When not swimming, she loves art, babysitting, and spending time with her family and friends.

Tenacity goes a long way in overcoming obstacles and a bloated ego

SWIMMING WITH THE TEN-AND-UNDERS AS A TEEN
Kathy Pride

What am I doing here? I asked myself as I tentatively dipped my big toe in the water to monitor its temperature. I looked out over my assigned lane and saw several bodies, *small* bodies, rhythmically churning through the water.

They were ten. I was fourteen. They knew how to do flip turns. I knew nothing except that one person had suggested I was a decent swimmer and ought to join a team.

Never underestimate the power of a positive statement. I was counting on those affirming words to get me through the next hour and a half.

I dipped my toe in the water one more time, waiting for the group to finish what they were doing. I wasn't sure what to expect, or even if I would swim the day I went to meet the coach. But somehow there I was, a fourteen-year-old who had been rather full of herself now standing over a lane filled with ten-year-olds who could beat the snot out of me. My self-assurance deflated rapidly. *Too bad*, I thought to myself; anything that could have helped me stay afloat would have been helpful at this point.

Not one to quit, I asked one of the swimmers what they were doing. "Ten 50's drill-kick, best stroke on ten seconds" was the reply. *Huh?* I knew I needed to learn about different strokes, but no one said anything about learning a foreign language.

Breaststroke was my stroke that had been noticed. A lifeguard at the JCC where I enjoyed splashing around on weekends told me I was a natural and pulled out a stopwatch one day to time me, and so started my competitive swimming career. First I entered small JCC meets, but soon I yearned for more, and more is what I got.

When I made the transition to USS swimming (AAU back then), all of a sudden I became an oversized little fish in a big, big pool. My ability was better matched to the tens than to the teens, so that is where I started. I had so much to learn! Best stroke? I only had one stroke. My freestyle truly was "free" style, and the only thing about my backstroke that was correct was that I was in fact on my back.

But weeks turned into months, and I didn't stay with the tens long. Soon I was training with my peers and moved from "C" meets to "A-B" meets on to state championships and beyond. I competed on my high school team (no separate girls' team, had to race against the boys) and now *I* was beating the snot out of some of those I swam with, and they were guys! The tenacity of not being turned off by swimming with the younger group was paying off.

I continued to swim through my first two years in college and ended up competing at the national meet and earned All-American honors. Not bad for a kid who began swimming because of a positive comment from a lifeguard and who remained undaunted by starting out with kids much younger (but faster).

Tenacity paid off. The only thought going through my mind the first day I showed up for "real" practice was *what am I doing here?* Now I'm grateful I had the tenacity to stick with it, stretching my preconceived notions of what I was capable of. Who would have thought!

"The man who is swimming against the stream knows the strength of it." ~Woodrow Wilson

Kathy Pride wears many hats, including the stressed-out diva tiara (www.divacelebration.com) and bathing cap as a triathlete and Masters swimmer. She lives in central Pennsylvania with her husband and four children where she blogs daily at www.kathypride.com. She is also an encourager, writer, and speaker. Join the conversation!

Section 4
Poolside Stories: Families, Friends, and Teammates

Isaiah 41:10

*So do not fear, for I am with you;
do not be dismayed, for I am your God.
I will strengthen you and help you;
I will uphold you with my righteous right hand.*

THE SWIM LESSON
Bryan Schalesky
as told to Marlo Schalesky

S mall arms squeezed my neck so hard I thought I would choke. A small body shivered and shook against me. Her grip grew tighter.

I sighed and waded into shallower water. Waves lapped the sides of the pool as other kids swam and leaped and turned somersaults in the water. Shouts of laughter rippled over the pool's surface. I pulled gently at my daughter's arm. "Loosen up, sweetheart. I won't let go of you."

"Nooooo." Bethany's whimper grew louder as she dug her fingers deeper into my skin.

"Swimming is fun. But you've got to let go of Daddy."

"I'm s-s-scared." Her teeth chattered even though the water was a balmy 80 degrees.

I swallowed and attempted to loosen her grip enough for me to breathe. But Bethany only grabbed harder, not because she loved me or wanted to be close to me, but only because she was afraid. This was our third swimming lesson and she still wasn't brave enough to let go. I reached for her goggles and put them on her, adjusting them so they fit just right. "Okay, are you ready to try?"

"I d-d-don't know."

I looked into her goggle-clad eyes. "You have to trust me. I'm right here. Trust me."

She took a deep breath.

"Trust me," I repeated again.

This time, Bethany nodded. "Okay, Daddy." Her grip loosened a little bit. Then a little bit more. And a little more.

I sidled toward the edge of the pool, then took her hands and placed them on the edge. Next I stepped back until I stood three feet away. "Push off and swim to me. You can do it."

Bethany studied the distance.

I reached out with both hands.

With a push and a splash, she was in the water on her own, then in my arms again.

I laughed. "You did it!"

She laughed back. "That was fun!"

"You want to go under the water?"

Her brows bunched in a frown.

I smiled. "Trust me."

Bethany straightened her shoulders. "I'm ready."

And down we went. Once. Twice. Three times. By the end of the lesson, Bethany had discovered a whole new world of fun and adventure. She could go underwater and look around. She could "sit" on the bottom of the pool for a whole three seconds. And she could kick her way from the edge all the way to me without being afraid. Swimming had ceased to be scary and instead was a joy. For an hour we swam and played and enjoyed every minute. Finally, it was time to leave.

"That was great, Daddy," Bethany exclaimed as she clamored out of the pool. "Can we come back tomorrow? And the day after that? And the day after that?"

I chuckled. "We'll come back soon. I promise."

"Yay!"

I grinned as I watched her scamper into the locker room. What a difference between the shivering, shaking girl who had climbed into the pool and the happy, exuberant girl who had climbed out. And it was all because she had decided to put aside fear and instead trust her daddy.

In some ways, my life with God is not much different from Bethany's swim lessons. Romans 8:15 says, "For you did not receive a spirit that makes you a slave again to fear, but you received the Spirit of sonship. And by him we cry, 'Abba, Father.'" When God calls me to try new things, to stretch past my comfort zone, to step out into the unknown, it's easy for me too to cling to Him out of fear. But God doesn't want me to grab onto Him because I'm afraid. Rather, He wants me to trust Him enough to let go of fear and embrace all the adventures He has for me. He wants me to learn to live in joy and freedom, to learn how to swim with Him.

And just like Bethany, I need to loosen my grip and trust God to be there if the waters get too deep.

May the God of hope fill you with all joy and peace as you trust in him, so that you may overflow with hope by the power of the Holy Spirit. – Romans 15:13

Marlo Schalesky is the award-winning author of hundreds of articles and numerous books, including her latest novel, *If Tomorrow Never Comes*, the second of her new "Love Stories with a Twist!" series. She lives in California with her swimmer husband and five young children. Find out more about Marlo at www.marloschalesky.com.

THE NEAR MISS
Kate Wilt

The sun was shining brightly in Ft. Lauderdale, Florida, on the day of my last race for my YMCA swim team. Short-course nationals was a great way to say goodbye to the sport that had given me so much, and I was excited to try out a relatively new event – the 200 breaststroke, which I had only swum three times before (qualifying for nationals on the third attempt). I was the only athlete from my team who had made the nationals time standard, so it was just my coach and me on the pool deck enjoying the gentle ocean breeze.

Yes, the sun was shining brightly – too brightly. By nine in the morning, it was 80 degrees and climbing. My hometown in central Pennsylvania had an average temperature of 20 degrees all winter, and my body was unaccustomed to such intense heat. Not wanting to exhaust my muscles before I even had the chance to swim, my coach suggested we visit the nearby International Swimming Hall of Fame. It was air-conditioned, and we had at least an hour and a half before my event was called, so we soon found ourselves sitting in the cool interior of the Hall, debating topics from stroke technique to my college prospects to the World War II air raids. After about half an hour, my coach said he wanted me to warm up a little bit in the pool, to make sure my body didn't get too tight from sitting. As we moseyed back to the aquatics complex, we heard something horrible:

"*And in this heat of the 200 breaststroke, we have, in Lane 1....*"

My coach starting sprinting to the blocks, and I dropped my bag and stripped down to my suit in a panic. I had no idea what heat was in the pool, or if I had already missed my swim, but I knew I wanted to be ready for anything. Everything was moving in slow motion, almost like witnessing a car accident. A million thoughts ran through my head – *Did I come all the way to Florida just to miss my event? Is my senior year going to end in a disappointment of this magnitude?* – I steeled myself to look at the scoreboard to find out which heat was in the pool.

Amazingly, it was only the second heat, but I was in heat four. I had no time to warm up and barely enough time to make it to my lane for the whistle indicating that we should step up on the blocks. For the first and only time in my eight-year career as a swimmer, I saw my coach get flustered. He kept telling me to do jumping jacks, stretch, loosen up, and raise my heart rate in the few seconds I had before I was told to step up. As it was, my heart was pounding plenty hard already and I couldn't do much but slump over in relief and residual fear. The next two minutes were surreal; as the whistle was blown we heard "take your marks," and the tone sounded that indicated the start of the race.

As I dove in the water, I have to admit that I wasn't thinking about my race strategy, my hand position, or my stroke count. I was filled with only thankfulness and amazement – I had not missed my race. Five more minutes in the Hall of Fame, and I would have gone home without swimming. The fact that I had almost failed to attend the biggest race of the year made me appreciate the experience so much more. I thought about the training that I had put in to get to nationals, about the two-a-day practices, the endless laps of breaststroke, the sore knees, the "off" meets where nothing goes right, and the eight years spent in love with the water. I thought about my amazing swim career, filled with laughter and tears.

Amazingly, there was no better way for me to finish my senior year than by almost missing my event; it made everything that followed that much sweeter. After the first length of the 200, my thoughts became more ordered and I was able to focus on the task at hand. My training kicked in, and I was able to finish with a personal best time, even though I hadn't warmed up, stretched, or even concentrated on my swim prior to hitting the water. I finished more than twenty places higher than I was seeded.

I couldn't talk about the race for days after the fact – I was still too shaken by my near-miss. It turns out that a simple mathematical error led to our miscalculation of the amount of time we had left to wait, and it was by sheer chance that we walked on deck at the exact right time. The experience was terrifying, and I would never want to repeat it, but it allowed me to say a truly appreciative goodbye to my amazing career as a swimmer.

Trust in him at all times, O people; pour out your hearts to him, for God is our refuge. – Psalm 62:8

Kate Wilt currently attends and swims for Grove City College in Pennsylvania. She recently broke the team record for the 200-yard breaststroke, the event that she thinks hurts more than anything in the world. She is crazy about water in all forms and sometimes stops by the pool late at night just to look through the window at the place she loves most. You can contact her at WiltKM1@gcc.edu.

REST FOR THE WEARY
Kathy Pride

"Hey, quit splashing me!" Chris, also known as Toad, said, a huge grin on his face. Life was good. After all, it was taper time and rest was abundant, giving teammates added time to revel in the hard work of the season and have some fun. The swimming in practice was hard and intense, but the rest was the best.

"Nah, why should I?" answered Nate, punctuating his words with sprays of water shot at Toad from between pursed lips. Then he splashed more water with his hands, shooting it toward Toad.

Andy and Aaron, the two other members of the boys' medley relay, joined in the fun, belly flopping and splashing water in every direction.

It looked more like a toddler pool party than a high school swim practice preparing for district championships in which they were the favored top seed.

Ah, the end of the season, taper time, when all the hard work of the previous six months would be capped off with shorter practices full of fun, rest, and low but high-intensity yardage.

The quartet had mastered the fun part, goofing off in the spirit of team camaraderie. They were a team, and if they finished first at the district meet they would advance to states.

"How was practice?" I asked Toad as he walked through the door almost forty minutes earlier than he had for the previous five months.

"Practice was great! We had tons of fun. Oh, and I feel really good in the water too." He walked over toward the kitchen counter and grabbed three chocolate chip cookies off a plate. "I love tapering," he added, his words muffled by a mouthful of cookie. "It feels so good to rest and have fun with the guys. The payoff is coming, I feel it. We're gonna win tomorrow, I know it," he continued, grabbing another cookie.

Rest for the weary so they could experience victory. And experience victory they did, both at districts and as teammates enjoying each other's friendship.

SWIMMING FUEL — Toad became a huge fan of pre-meet chocolate chip cookies because of the strong association he had with eating the cookies prior to districts and the fun and victory he and his relay team experienced.

Kathy Pride wears many hats, including the stressed-out diva tiara (www.divacelebration.com) and bathing cap as a triathlete and Masters swimmer. She lives in central Pennsylvania with her husband and four children where she blogs daily at www.kathypride.com. She is also an encourager, writer, and speaker. Join the conversation!

The Far Side of the Pool
Marlo Schalesky

Bryan and I stood at the edge of the community pool and watched the water lap into the gutters. Two teenagers splashed at the far end while an old man slowly made his way back and forth in the last lane.

I crossed my arms over my chest. "They have lessons for preschoolers. Bethany's old enough now."

Bryan scowled. "Are you kidding? There's no way I'm having a stranger teach my daughter to swim."

"You're going to do it?" I cleared my throat. "Do you know how?"

Bryan raised his eyebrows.

"I know, I know. You swam for Stanford, went to the NCAA, still have swim records on the books back in North Dakota." I jabbed my finger into his chest. "But that doesn't mean you know how to teach a little kid to swim."

He squatted down and dangled his fingers in the water. "Eighty-one degrees. Exactly." He grinned up at me. "Didn't I tell you about the summer when I was twelve?"

"Of course." I knew all about that summer, or at least I thought so. I'd heard the story a hundred times – how Bryan had gone flying off the front end of his brand-new 10-speed. How his left arm swelled like a sausage. How his mother insisted that the doctors X-ray the other arm as well, only to find that both arms were broken. Broken and put into twin casts during the summer he was supposed to break the state records for the twelve-and-under age group and lead his team to the state championships. Broken arms, broken dreams.

"So you know what I did that summer?"

"Well, you didn't swim. You didn't break any records. You didn't win the state championship."

"Yes I did."

"What?"

"I helped win the state championship."

"How?"

"The coach put me in charge of the littlest kids. He didn't have time to teach them. But I did. I had all summer." Bryan gazed over the pool. A smile twitched his lips. "I taught over a dozen little kids to make it from one end of the pool to the other. And because of them we won the state championship that year. You wouldn't believe how many points those kids won just because they could swim across the pool."

"You never told me that."

He shook his head. "It wasn't always pretty, but it worked. And we won." His voice lowered. "Even without the team's 'big star.'" He stood and playfully flicked droplets of water over my shirt. "So I think I can teach our daughter how to swim."

I laughed. "Okay, I guess you're qualified."

Bryan rested his hand on my shoulder. "Glad you agree. Now let's go home."

We turned from the pool and walked back to the parking lot. As I got into our car and buckled my seatbelt, I glanced over to Bryan in the driver's seat. "You know, that is the most profound story I've heard in a long time."

"Huh?"

"Do you think it works like that in God's kingdom too?"

"What are you talking about?"

I rubbed my chin. "Well, I'm no superstar evangelist. I haven't brought thousands to Christ. I write books, but we both know they haven't rocketed up the bestseller lists."

Bryan stifled his cough.

I shot him a glare. "We don't have any big, successful ministry, and our small group is, well, small."

"It's good though."

"But we're not setting any records."

"Maybe we don't need to."

I settled back in my chair. Paul does say, "For what is our hope, our joy, or the crown in which we will glory in the presence of our Lord Jesus when he comes? Is it not you?" (1 Thessalonians 2:19).

"Just like those little kids were my crown in the state championships."

I nodded. "You know, I've been so worried that what I'm doing in God's kingdom isn't good enough. That somehow I'm falling short. But maybe it isn't about me and my success. Perhaps God's telling me that it's enough to help others learn how to get to the other side of the pool."

Bryan winked at me. "Sometimes that's what winning is all about."

Who do you think we're going to be proud of when our Master Jesus appears if it's not you? You're our pride and joy! — 1 Thessalonians 2:19, The Message.

Marlo Schalesky earned her master's degree in theology from Fuller Theological Seminary and lives in Salinas, California, with her swimmer husband and five young children. She is the award-winning author of hundreds of articles and numerous books, including her latest novel, *If Tomorrow Never Comes*, the second of her new "Love Stories with a Twist!" series. Find out more about Marlo at www.marloschalesky.com.

Section 5
DQ'd

Every swimmer has experienced being disqualified.
Do you remember your first, your funniest, your most recent, your most embarrassing?

Numbers 15:15

*The community is to have the same rules for you
and for the alien living among
you; this is a lasting ordinance for the generations to come.
You and the alien shall be the same before the LORD.*

Raised in a Christian household filled with laughter, writer and artist Cuyler Black knows God has a great sense of humor. One of his favorite Bible verses is Genesis 21:6: "God has brought me laughter." Growing up in Ottawa, Ontario, the son of a seventh-generation minister and a musical-comedy actress, Cuyler began cartooning at an early age. His unique ministry of Inherit the Mirth® is founded on the belief that God has a sense of humor and that positive laughter can improve health and spread joy throughout the world. Cuyler is a fun, dynamic communicator who is available to speak on topics related to faith and humor. He resides in Danbury, Connecticut. Be ready to laugh when you check out his website: www.inheritthemirth.com.

PLAYING BY THE RULES
Kathy Pride

The victory was sweet: League Swimming Championships, and the motley group of swimmers had just touched out their opponent for the victory. This victory was particularly sweet as during the regular dual meet season the group of four had lost twice by a similar margin to the same team.

Finally this group of four swimmers with shaved heads, sleek body suits, and the latest in high-tech competitive swimwear had beaten their arch rival. Today they were victorious, or so they thought when the anchor swimmer out-touched the opponent at the wall, his left arm blasting out of the water fist clenched, signifying victory.

But he hadn't seen the official make the call. Somehow his teammates also missed the call. They were too absorbed in the battle of churning arms and kicking feet to notice the official's raised arm signaling the DQ.

The victory was no longer theirs, they had broken the rules. One of the swimmers had exploded off the block in anticipation of the next swimmer's touch, his timing off by a fraction. Elation evaporated into disappointment. They had been so close, but once again today the victory was elusive. The elation they experienced was soon replaced by shock and disappointment. They had been so close—then the excuses and blame followed.

But the coach wouldn't put up with excuses and blame. It was just one of those things. "Sure it hurts," said the coach, acknowledging the frustration the swimmers felt at being so close to knocking off their arch rival. "But how would you feel if they had won by an unfair advantage? You wouldn't have wanted them to beat you because of a jump start, would you?" They had to agree it would have erased the sweetness of the victory.

Finally, one of the four broke the silence. "Well, I guess we'd better work on our starts some more before districts." The first concession was followed by another. "Yeah, we need to be tight and not single one of us out, we're a team…I could have missed my turn…." And finally, "Yeah, we know we can do it, and coach, you're right, we want to beat them fair and square, so we'll just go after them at districts."

It's never easy to be disqualified, but playing by the rules always yields the sweetest victory.

Similarly if anyone competes as an athlete he does not receive the victor's crown unless he competes according to the rules.
— 2 Timothy 2:5

Kathy Pride wears many hats, including the stressed-out diva tiara (www.divacelebration.com) and bathing cap as a triathlete and Masters swimmer. She lives in central Pennsylvania with her husband and four children where she blogs daily at www.kathypride.com. She is also an encourager, writer, and speaker. Join the conversation!

MY FIRST SWIM MEET AT EIGHT YEARS OLD
Alexandria Mangas

Everyone has to experience their first swim meet. They have to get through their first race, their first DQ (disqualification), and their first miss/scratch of an event. Like all swimmers, my first swim meet was nerve-wracking. At eight years old I walked onto the pool deck, and even though it was a home meet everything seemed foreign: two hundred kids roaming the deck, loud music, officials watching every breath and every stroke. I joined my team camping on the deck next to the announcer's booth. I was very timid and this meet wasn't helping. I whispered a silent prayer, and suddenly I found one of my only friends on the team, Rose. It was her first meet too, and soon we began talking about all the things that could possibly go wrong but also all the good things that come with the bad. For example, if you get DQ'd you get Dairy Queen (ice cream). If you don't make it back for finals, you get to do whatever you want for the rest of the day, etc.

We were having such a good time talking, it didn't even faze us when we heard the call for girls eight and under backstroke. Five minutes later our coach came running up to us, yelling something that sounded like, *"Girls, you missed your event! What are you doing!"* Suddenly we realized we had missed our first event, an hour later we had to swim our 100 freestyle, laughing all the way up to the block, and we were not the least bit nervous. Somehow I think that was an answer to prayer (though Rose and I had to do a "punishment set" for missing the event).

"In swimming, the trick to winning is simply to touch the wall first." — Unknown

Aly Mangas is a senior swim captain at Covenant Christian High School in Indianapolis, Indiana. She loves the smell of chlorine, carb loading, tapering, finding drag tights, and the 200 fly. Not bad for a girl who used to scream when she got water on her face during bath time as a toddler. In addition to the life-lessons she has learned from swimming, Aly has had an education of the heart the past three summers — building a house and orphanage in Juarez, Mexico with Casas Por Cristo, and teaching a media workshop to fellow high school students in Thailand with Good News Productions.

Section 6
Hearing His Voice in the Water

John 10:27

*My sheep listen to my voice;
I know them, and they follow me.*

What God Has to Say
Moire Yue (18)

I am currently reading some of Rob Bell's work, and I keep hearing this recurring statement: "This is really about that." It seems that this statement can't possibly relate to swimming, but I can assure you it does. This assurance comes from a personal experience that ultimately gave me a greater sense of trust in God.

During my junior year season of high school swimming, I peaked, and it seemed almost weird how much I improved. But God was planning something big, and this was just the precursor. At the beginning of the season, I sat on a 200 IM time of 2:17. But by state, I had dropped to 2:08, a time that was considered very fast for my team. Unfortunately, I had bad shoulder pain after the season ended. I went in for an MRI and was diagnosed with mild tendinitis in both shoulders. I blamed it on the hard training I had done that past season.

I entered a physical therapy rehabilitation program but was soon diagnosed with a partial thickness rotator cuff tear – something my doctor had never seen in a sixteen-year-old before. The physical therapist told me I could only kick for the spring/summer season.

When fall of my senior year came, I wanted to swim the high school season because I had been voted captain. However, my physical therapist told me my injury hadn't healed as much as he expected, so he advised me to sit out on the first eight meets. That way I could swim sections and state with more recovered shoulders.

In frustration, I couldn't understand what God was doing and blamed Him. Going into sections, I was discouraged because our team lost conference, and I had been unable to help out. I thought I was a useless captain because I wasn't being a leader in the water. But after observing many meets from the deck, I realized that being a leader is more than just fast swims. It's about character. It's about the circumstances and how we deal with them. And I finally understood. God had blessed me with fast times – but He gave me an even greater blessing by taking them away. He had snatched them from my grip to challenge me so I could experience what it meant to be a true leader.

During state finals, I was put in all three relays and the 100 backstroke. What happened that night was the Lord's doing, because what I accomplished could not have been done without His help. My 200 medley relay not only won the event, but we earned an All-American award for our time and broke our twenty-year school record. After that event, none of the other races mattered. I just swam the rest of the meet glorifying God because of the accomplishment He gave to me. I began to see the plan He had all along. My fast times had been taken away so that I would learn to put my trust in God's timing instead of my own. If I learn to be patient with God, He will reward me with everything I need. However, faith is necessary to trust Him with what I don't know or control. Once I let go of the control I yearned for concerning my shoulders, I received the blessing of having my last high school season be my most enjoyable one.

So you see, *this* is really about *that*. Captainship is really about character. Trust is really about faith. Swimming is really about God, and therefore God's glory.

Now, faith is being sure of what we hope for and certain of what we do not see. — Hebrews 11:1

"This is really about that." ~Rob Bell

Moire Yue is a freshman swimmer at Wheaton College in Illinois. Growing up in Edina, a small suburb outside the Twin Cities, Minnesota, she began swimming when she was ten, but not competitively until she was fourteen. Her favorite events include the 200 IM and the 100 free, but she has been swimming backstroke for the Wheaton Thunder. Feel free to contact her at moire.yue@my.wheaton.edu.

MY PRAYER CLOSET IS 25 YARDS LONG
Beverly Bush Smith

When we pray, Jesus tells us in the King James Version of Matthew 6, we should enter our "closet," close the door, and pray to the Father in secret.

I definitely had a problem if I took that literally. Every closet in our home bulged with clothing, cartons, books, and treasures from our boys such as snakeskins and skateboards.

Even the bathroom failed to offer safe recluse, with someone always needing a hair dryer, shampoo, or the scales. And when I was alone in the house, the phone, doorbell, cat, and dog inevitably interrupted or distracted me.

Then one morning as I hurried to clean up after breakfast, I realized I had the perfect place, the perfect block of time for prayer. Trouble was, I'd labeled it "fitness time." Yet every day I headed for our neighborhood pool to swim my laps. Why not make this "thing for my body" a "thing for the spirit"?

In the pool, I'm essentially alone. Even in the busy season a lane line separates me from the "Marco Polo" players and other lap swimmers.

Here, as I follow the blue tiled line on the bottom of the pool, no one can ask my advice, permission, or opinion. They can't even ask to borrow anything. And, praise God, I cannot hear the phone and doorbell ring!

The swimming pool became my 25-yard long "closet" for prayer and meditation on that day more than thirty years ago. It still is all through the year.

Because I lose track when I try to count laps, I pray through the alphabet, allowing each letter to trigger a new prayer. Sometimes my entire focus is praise and thanksgiving. I begin with praise for my <u>A</u>donai. I thank Him for such little <u>blessings</u> as the silken feel of the water flowing past and its refreshing coolness.

I give thanks for my <u>h</u>ealth—that I'm able to keep swimming now that I'm an octogenarian. I thank Him that just as the water <u>supports</u> me, underneath are His everlasting arms. And, swimming backstroke, I praise Him for the beauty of His <u>u</u>niverse, surveying the blue of His heavens, punctuated with seagulls in flight, softened by downy clouds.

Other times I salt the water with my tears as I pray <u>healing</u> for a friend with cancer, <u>discernment</u> in a desperate financial situation, or <u>s</u>alvation for family members.

Sometimes I wrestle with my own stubborn will and pride, knowing there's a particular facet of my life I continue to cling to –something I should give over to the Lord.

Some days I sing hymns or praise songs to myself, exhaling bubbles to the rhythm of "<u>Be</u> exalted, O Lord," "<u>Ho</u>ly, holy, holy!" and especially when I swim early, "<u>When</u> Morning Gilds the Skies."

Often I use the letter of the lap to trigger my recall of favorite scriptures. "May the meditations of my heart be

<u>a</u><u>cceptable</u> to You"... "<u>B</u><u>e</u> still and know that I am God"... ."<u>C</u><u>ome</u> unto Me, all you who labor and are heavy laden."

Sometimes, I admit, I become so absorbed in the scripture or my prayers that I lose track of how many laps I've swum. Not to worry. Nothing's wasted (that's a "w" lap) in God's economy.

And I never fail to leave my watery "closet" cleansed, refreshed, and with new spiritual and physical <u>z</u><u>est</u>.

Devote yourselves to prayer, being watchful and thankful.
– Colossians 4:2, NIV

Eighty-something Beverly Bush Smith describes herself as a "late bloomer" who began her Christian walk in her forties and started writing books on her way past fifty. She has published five books (fiction: *Wings of a Dove* and *Evidence of Things Unseen*; nonfiction: *Uniquely You, Change for the Better,* and *Caught in the Middle*) and more than five hundred articles.

AM I A SWIMMER?
Melanie LeBaron

I swam today for the first time in twenty-five years. I mean really swam. Not bobbing around in a hotel swimming pool where you can barely manage three strokes before hitting the far side, but laps in a real 25-meter pool at a brand-new health club.

"I joined during the pre-construction sale but have never been here before," I mentioned as I checked in with the friendly receptionist.

"Would you like someone to show you around?" she asked. As I nodded, she waved over a fit young man who led me into the club.

"What are you most interested in? Cardio, the pool. . .?"

"Yes, the pool. I'm a swimmer."

Did I really say that? I immediately thought. I'm not a swimmer at all! I'm a forty-six-year-old slightly overweight woman who took beginning swimming in college and then occasionally swam leisurely laps until graduation ended my access to a pool. Even then I was never a strong swimmer and out of breath after a few laps. Now that I told this personal trainer dude I'm a swimmer, I bet he thinks I must be good at it. Maybe even a competitive swimmer in an older adult category. Isn't the definition of a swimmer one who swims? Can you opt out for twenty-five years and still call yourself a swimmer?

Once in the pool, my body relaxed until I realized the strokes were not flowing as naturally as they should. I resisted putting my face in the water for the breaststroke, and my sidestroke was a mass of flailing appendages. When I noticed the personal trainers' desks were located behind the pool windows I became even more self-conscious. I wondered if the guy who showed me around was watching and chuckling about my declaration, "I'm a swimmer."

I wasn't self-conscious when I swam years ago. In fact, swimming was how I could lose myself—just floating and gliding away from my "problems" and college-girl angst. I would sing music in my head to the rhythm of my strokes, memorizing hymns and praise songs day by day, line by line. Meditating on those peaceful songs as I splashed through the water kept me sane when I suffered a broken engagement my last semester. I can still hear the strokes beating the rhythm as I sang "Seek ye first the kingdom of God…" over and over as the water washed away my tears.

"Where did you buy your swim gloves?" I asked a woman while we were toweling off.

"At Dick's."

"Do they have swim caps?"

"Yes, and I think there's also a swim store about a mile up the highway that I'm going to check out. I stopped swimming about ten years ago and really need to start back up."

"Me too!"

It's such a common thing to neglect doing what we love. Why do we give up on the passions of our youth as we get older? The obvious answer is the urgent necessities of life crowd out the very things that used to give us life. The more subtle answer is sometimes we forget who we are.

As a child, my family spent summers traveling and loved to swim in motel pools. In fact, we wouldn't stay at any motel without a pool. As a family of unathletically-inclined readers, we didn't regularly watch sports on TV, yet we always watched the swimming events during the Olympics. So taking swimming lessons in college was the fulfillment of a lifelong yearning in me. Maybe swimming appealed to me because it's a more individual sport. Maybe chlorine was in my blood from all those idyllic summers on family vacations. But then I graduated and grew up and stopped nurturing my childhood love for swimming—other than still insisting on motels with pools.

God loves to see us pursue our passions and unique talents; after all He created us to enjoy doing certain things. He reminds us repeatedly that we are His own precious children—knights and princesses of His kingdom. I believe it delights Him to see us "playing" with the talents and interests He gave us. But it must be easy to wander from the playground, because He also warns us not to forget who we are (James 1:23-24). In Romans 12:6-8 (NLT), Paul encourages us to remember to use our gifts to our best ability: "If you are a teacher, teach well."

Of course, interests change and some dreams even die to be replaced by others. Certain seasons of life make it a challenge to pursue your passion. But if you're a singer, sing a lullaby. If a writer, write a card to a shut-in. If a model railroader, run trains with a scout troop. If someday you no longer have regular access to a pool, it does not mean you aren't still a swimmer deep down in your heart at the core of your being. And competitive swimmers, just because you've made it as far as you can, or graduate and no longer are on a team, or have injuries that prevent certain strokes, that does not mean you are no longer a swimmer. Whenever you can, however life buffets and changes you, if you're a swimmer, swim.

Tonight as I contemplate my inaugural health club swim, I lie in bed wide awake, feeling a little sore, wondering if I will ever regain that selfless gliding meditative state. As visions of shopping for Esther Williams swim caps dance in my head, I remember my childhood and think to myself, *Yes, I am a swimmer.*

Delight yourself in the LORD and he will give you the desires of your heart. – Psalm 37:4

Melanie LeBaron lives in Indianapolis, Indiana, with her husband of twenty-four years, Jeff. She enjoys songwriting, freelance writing/editing (www.wingmaneditorial.com), and volunteering as a church librarian. She has a B.A. degree in music from Central College, Pella, Iowa, and an M.S. degree in library science from the University of Illinois, Urbana.

A Breath of Encouragement
Judith Ann Squier

S wimming was a lifesaver for me, the little girl born without legs. No sitting on the sidelines watching the long-legged kids have all the fun. I could swim like a fish from day one. And swim I did at the public pool on 100-degree days. My ascent up the ladder to the high dive made the actual plunge anticlimactic.

Swimming was the highlight for a decade of summers during my month-long stay at a camp for crippled children. I prided myself in being out front as our group of disabled swimmers did the annual 2-mile lake swim. And in my keepsake album I still treasure my certificates in advanced swimming and junior lifesaving.

My swimming career peaked in college, when I competed in the National Paralympics receiving silver medals for the front crawl, breaststroke and backstroke.

But my swimming essentially evaporated in adulthood. Some might say I was busy with other things. Others might offer the excuse that I didn't have a pool nearby, but the truth was our property adjoined the town's swim club. Summer afternoons found me sitting poolside in my wheelchair, watching my three daughters having all the fun. Never did I dream of jumping in myself. Go public with my deformed body? Are you kidding?

Then came the summer when, overheated and overweight, at a weak moment I said yes to my daughters' urging to partake of a cool evening dip. Respecting my self-consciousness, they preceded me through the gate, checking out the pool, then gave me the green light: no kids were anywhere to be seen. That summer the fish mama was resurrected. I'd swim at seven in the morning or at dusk, always careful to avoid becoming the spectacle.

Some people overcome their fears. I've made it through a lot of them but not this one. It still hurts to hear kids say, "Look, Mom, she has no legs."

Actually I've come to realize life's pain has driven me to a lifesaving dependence on God, my Maker. I never asked Him to heal me. I was content that He was with me in life's rough waters. He in me and I in Him. Some mornings, when I'd swim as the sun came up over the hill, I'd see my shadow in the next lane and think to myself, *That's Jesus swimming beside me.*

One evening I wheeled out of the women's dressing room into a conversation between another swimmer and the club's custodian. The troubled mom was nursing her aching back in the steaming hot tub. I stopped in my tracks as I heard the hymn-humming custodian's testimonial: "The degree of our faith determines our well-being. I prayed without ceasing about my back problem. I claimed God's promises. Now look at me, I'm all better."

Sitting legless in my wheelchair, ready to jump into the pool, I jumped into the conversation. Flinging my arms heavenward, I looked the insensitive man in the eye and said: "When God doesn't heal us, He inhabits us!"

Yep, Jesus and me, we're a team. He's always there with me – the Master Swimmer who indwells me, affirms me, and empowers me to get out there no matter what. And together we provide the world with a breath of encouragement.

As the Father has loved me, so have I loved you. Now remain in my love. – John 15:9

Judith Ann (Judy) Squier has learned firsthand about God's power made perfect in human weakness. Born without legs, she has lived not an ordinary but an extraordinary life. Her writing and her public speaking embody God's specialty – transforming broken people into sources of healing and blessing. Judy and her husband David reside in Grants Pass, Oregon. You can reach her via email at judyann777@aol.com or visit her website: squierfamily.net/Judy.HTML

A Final Letter to His Senior Swimmers

Coach Jon Lederhouse

To the senior class of Wheaton Swimmers 2008, upon the occasion of your final CCIW Championships:

Congratulations on a most memorable four years of athletic endeavor. How quickly in hindsight these past four seasons have made their way through our lives. By shear numbers, personality, and performances you have impacted your teammates, coaches and opponents during this time. I am so thankful to have had you all aboard and to have been able to be a part of these, your memories.

As you conclude your CCIW career this weekend, make sure to take the time to "implant" the memories of this meet and your shared experiences with all these teammates, friends, and family present. Never again in your life will you have this kind of athletic experience, so savor it to the fullest. Never again will you be blessed (or cursed) to hear the phrase…

- "take your marks"
- "what time is it?"
- "good effort"
- or even "…but you can beat him with a stick" ☺

Let me take this final opportunity as your official coach (though, of course, you will always remain "my swimmers" and I will always know your best times!) to pass on a reminder from a devotion you may have heard from me during previous seasons:

Many coaches say, "It's not how you start but how you finish that counts." Given the amount of time I have dedicated during swim practice to improving your racing starts, you know that I think it IS important how you start. However, how you finish is the MOST important thing. To that end, let us reconsider one of the famous aquatics portions of Scripture:

> Immediately Jesus made the disciples get into the boat and go on ahead of him to the other side, while he dismissed the crowd. After he had dismissed them, he went up on a mountainside by himself to pray. When evening came, he was there alone, but the boat was already a considerable distance from land, buffeted by the waves because the wind was against it. During the fourth watch of the night Jesus went out to them, walking on the lake. When the disciples saw him walking on the lake, they were terrified. "It's a ghost," they said, and cried out in fear. But Jesus immediately said to them: "Take courage! It is I. Don't be afraid." "Lord, if it's you," Peter replied, "tell me to come to you on the water." "Come," he said. Then Peter got down out of the boat, walked on the water and came toward Jesus. But when he saw the wind, he was afraid and, beginning to sink, cried

out, "Lord, save me!" Immediately Jesus reached out his hand and caught him. "You of little faith," he said, "why did you doubt?" And when they climbed into the boat, the wind died down. Then those who were in the boat worshiped him, saying, "Truly you are the Son of God."

Matthew 14:22-32

Although you may feel a bit old this weekend, in reality you are still only at the start of your life, a life that God can use for great things for His kingdom. But take note of Peter in this passage, who did begin well in faith, stepping out of the boat onto the water. Yet he forgot the *most important* aspect of Christian faith and that is:

FINISHING WELL REQUIRES THE PROPER FOCUS:
Distractions will come...fears will come...thus you must always keep your eyes on Jesus, the author and finisher of your faith. Spiritually we SINK when we put our eyes on ourselves or externals, shifting the focus away from Jesus.

If you remember nothing else from your Wheaton swimming career, remember just this:
"NEVER GIVE UP...NEVER SURRENDER"...NEVER TAKE YOUR EYES OFF CHRIST
And you will finish well

I have fought the good fight, I have finished the race, I have kept the faith. Now there is in store for me the crown of righteousness, which the Lord, the righteous Judge, will award to me on that day—and not only to me, but also to all who have longed for his appearing. — 2 Timothy 4:7-8

Wheaton has enjoyed twelve top-ten national finishes by its men's team and eight by its women's team and more. The 2008-09 season will be the thirty-third for Jon Lederhouse as head swimming coach and aquatics director at Wheaton College. During this time Wheaton teams have established themselves as the major small college swimming power in Illinois, consistently placing swimmers in the NCAA Division III National Championship finals. Jon and his wife, Jill, professor and chair of the Wheaton College Department of Education, have three children and reside in Wheaton. He can be contacted at: jonathan.e.lederhouse@wheaton.edu

Section 7
A Swim-bag Full of Goodies

Romans 15:4-5

*For everything that was written in the past
was written to teach us,
so that through endurance and the encouragement
of the Scriptures we might have hope.
May the God who gives endurance and encouragement give
you a spirit of unity among yourselves as you
follow Christ Jesus.*

Top Ten Q&A with Olympic Gold Medalist Sheila Taormina

Aly Mangas

Mangas: What is your favorite swim ritual?
Taormina: *A good warm-up with fast kicking and some holding the breath 50's.*

Mangas: How did swimming give you courage to forge into a new area as a pentathlete?
Taormina: *Learning the technique early is important, because swimming can be difficult if you learn it as an adult.*

Mangas: What is your favorite swimming memory?
Taormina: *My mom taking my twin brother and me to get donuts and hot chocolate after the freezing morning outdoor early summer workouts when there was no heat in the pool in Michigan.*

Mangas: What advice would you give a middle and high school student?
Taormina: *If you want to work hard at a goal, then don't let peer pressure lead you astray. Some people will make fun of you for working hard, but just ignore them on the way to your dream.*

Mangas: What is your favorite swimming drill?
Taormina*: One-arm swimming with non-pulling arm at your side.*

Mangas: What is your favorite book?
Taormina: God's Joyful Runner *by Russell Ramsey (a biography on Eric Liddell, the runner from the 1924 Olympics . . . [The movie]* Chariots of Fire *is about his story.) I also love any John Steinbeck book, especially* The Moon Is Down, Cannery Row, The Grapes of Wrath, *and* East of Eden.

Mangas: What do you think about when you are training?
Taormina: *Technique, technique, technique.*

Mangas: Do you have a favorite swim training video?
Taormina*: I never owned one in my life. I studied underwater still photos of Mark Spitz, Rowdy Gaines, and Mary T. Meagher that Doc Counsilman took back in the '70's and printed booklets that he gave to each of his summer swim campers — my twin brother and I went to his camp when we were about twelve years old, and now the booklets are classic.*

Mangas: If you could go back and do it all over again, is there anything you would do differently?
Taormina: *Not really. Although had I known I would do pentathlon later in life, then perhaps a little time on a horse as a young girl would have been helpful.*

Mangas: What are your future dreams?
Taormina: *To take what I've learned and give back to others, while finding time to relax more than I do now.*

Olympic gold medalist Sheila Taormina became the first female athlete in the 112-year history of the modern Games to compete in four Olympics in three different sports. Check out Sheila's blog at http://www.SheliaT.com

Are You a Swimming Genius?
(Take the swimming trivia quiz to find out)

What are the four competitive swim strokes?

What does IM stand for?

Which U.S. president regularly swam nude in the Potomac River?

Which Olympics debuted the first marathon swim (a 10-kilometer, open-water race)?

If an official declares a swimmer as breaking a rule, the swimmer is what?

Which Olympics, held in the Stockholm, Sweden, harbor, marked the beginning of electronic timing?

Swimmers originally dove from the edge of the pool until diving blocks were incorporated at which Olympics?

When was the flip-turn developed?

What is the order of the individual medley?

Swimming was part of the first modern Summer Olympics in Athens in what year?

Which stroke was first a variation of breaststroke until it was accepted as a separate style in the 1952 Olympics?

Elephants are capable of swimming how far a day, using their trunks as natural snorkels?

Who invented swim fins?

What world-renowned Grammy musician broke a national swim record in Greece at the age of fourteen and even dreamed of becoming an Olympic swimmer?

Who was the first swimmer to set American records in all four racing strokes?

(see answers on next page)

"Are You a Swimming Genius" Answers

— Each correct answer rewards you with 1 point —

What are the four competitive swim strokes? (freestyle, butterfly, breaststroke, backstroke)

What does IM stand for? (individual medley)

Which U.S. president regularly swam nude in the Potomac River? (John Quincy Adams)

Which Olympics debuted the first marathon swim (a 10-kilometer, open-water race)? (The 2008 Beijing Olympics)

If an official declares a swimmer as breaking a rule, the swimmer is what? (DQ'd — disqualified)

Which Olympics, held in the Stockholm, Sweden, harbor, marked the beginning of electronic timing? (1912)

Swimmers originally dove from the edge of the pool until diving blocks were incorporated at which Olympics? (1936)

When was the flip-turn developed? (by the 1950s)

What is the order of the individual medley? (butterfly, backstroke, breaststroke, and freestyle)

Swimming was part of the first modern Summer Olympics in Athens in what year? (1896)

What stroke was first a variation of breaststroke until it was accepted as a separate style in the 1952 Olympics? (The butterfly)

Elephants are capable of swimming how far a day, using their trunks as natural snorkels? (20 miles)

Who invented swim fins? (Benjamin Franklin)

What world-renowned Grammy musician broke a national swim record in Greece at the age of fourteen and even dreamed of becoming an Olympic swimmer? (Yanni)

Who was the first swimmer to set American records in all four racing strokes? (Tracy Caulkins)

11-15 points – you are a swimming genius!
6-10 points – you are obviously a competitor!
1-5 points — Who cares? You obviously have more fun swimming laps than memorizing trivia.

Swim Quotes for Your Locker

"The man who is swimming against the stream knows the strength of it." ~Woodrow T. Wilson

"Breaststroke is an athletic event; butterfly is a political statement." ~Paul Tsongas

"Sometimes God calms the storm. At other times, He calms the sailor. And sometimes He makes us swim." ~Unknown

"No man drowns if he perseveres in praying to God, and can swim." ~Russian Proverb

"In the end, swimming is not about what you achieve, it is about who you become." ~Unknown

Great Bible Verses to Memorize While Swimming

Set your minds on things above, not on earthly things. – Colossians 3:2

All hard work brings a profit, but mere talk leads only to poverty. – Proverbs 14:23

And we know that in all things God works for the good of those who love him, who have been called according to his purpose.. – Romans 8:28

For the word of God is living and active. Sharper than any double-edged sword, it penetrates even to dividing soul and spirit, joints and marrow; it judges the thoughts and attitudes of the heart. – Hebrews 4:12

Trust in the LORD with all your heart and lean not on your own understanding; in all your ways acknowledge him, and he will make your paths straight. – Proverbs 3:5-6

The disciples went and woke him, saying, "Lord, save us! We're going to drown!" He replied, "You of little faith, why are you so afraid?" Then he got up and rebuked the winds and the waves, and it was completely calm. The men were amazed and asked, "What kind of man is this? Even the winds and the waves obey him!" – Matthew 8:25-27

But when he asks, he must believe and not doubt, because he who doubts is like a wave of the sea, blown and tossed by the wind. That man should not think he will receive anything from the Lord; he is a double-minded man, unstable in all he does.. – James 1:6-8

Be strong and very courageous. Be careful to obey all the law my servant Moses gave you; do not turn from it to the right or to the left, that you may be successful wherever you go. – Joshua 1:7

Finally, brothers, whatever is true, whatever is noble, whatever is right, whatever is pure, whatever is lovely, whatever is admirable—if anything is excellent or praiseworthy—think about such things. – Philippians 4:8

Commit to the LORD whatever you do, and your plans will succeed. – Proverbs 16:3

"For I know the plans I have for you," declares the LORD, "plans to prosper you and not to harm you, plans to give you hope and a future." – Jeremiah 29:11

About the Authors

Aly Mangas is a senior swim captain at Covenant Christian High School in Indianapolis, Indiana. She plans to swim in college and continue to swim for as long as she can. She loves the smell of chlorine, carb loading, tapering, finding drag tights, and the 200 fly. Not bad for a girl who used to scream when she got water on her face during bath time as a toddler.

Janet Hommel Mangas is a swim mom writer who loves the aroma of chlorine. A family/humor columnist for *The Daily Journal* in Johnson County, Indiana, she received her B.S. degree from Purdue University and M.A. degree from Cincinnati Christian Seminary, which has absolutely nothing to do with swimming. A popular speaker, she loves to tell stories, which could be one reason why all three daughters took up swimming.

I am not ashamed of the gospel,
because it is the power of God for the salvation of everyone
who believes.

Romans 1:16

What's Your Story?

If you were encouraged by *Oxygen for the Swimmer*, we would love to hear from you: Oxygenfortheswimmer@yahoo.com

If you would like to submit your story to *More Oxygen for the Swimmer,* email it to:
Oxygenfortheswimmer@yahoo.com

Or mail your story to:
Oxygen for the Swimmer
7077 Stones Crossing Road
Greenwood, IN 46143

CPSIA information can be obtained at www.ICGtesting.com
Printed in the USA
LVOW060745151211

259531LV00001B/166/P